COASTS
OF THE
BRITISH ISLES

Terry Jennings

Evans Brothers Limited

First published in 2001 by Evans Brothers Limited

Evans Brothers Ltd
2a Portman Mansions
Chiltern Street
London W1M 1LE

© Evans Brothers Limited 2001

Commissioned by: Su Swallow
Consultant: Stephen Watts
Series design: Neil Sayer
Editor: Debbie Fox
Picture research: Vicky Brooker and Julia Bird
Maps and diagrams: Hardlines

British Library Cataloguing in Publication Data.

Jennings, Terry
  Coastlines of the British Isles
  1.Coasts - British Isles - Juvenile literature
  I.Title
  551.4'57'0941

ISBN 0237522381

Printed in Dubai

ACKNOWLEDGEMENTS

For permission to reproduce copyright material, the author
and publishers gratefully acknowledge the following:

Cover Robert Harding Picture Library
page 7 Ecoscene **page 8** (left) Collections/Paul Watts (right)
Robert Harding Picture Library **page 9** RonaldToms/Oxford
Scientific Films **page 10** Collections/Paul Watts **page 11**
Collections/Alain Le Garsmeur **page 12** Ecoscene/
Gryniewicz **page 13** (top) Skyscan Photolibrary/Peter
Smith (bottom) Travel Ink/Chris North **page 14** (left)
Collections/Michael Diggin (right) Dr Terry Jennings **page
15** (left) Collections/Graeme Peacock (right) Collections/
Gena Davies **page 16** Ian West/Oxford Scientific Films **page
17** (left) Skyscan Photolibrary/R&R Photography (right)
Robert Harding Picture Library **page 18** Collections/Mike
Kipling **page 19** (top) Ecoscene/Tony Page (bottom) David
Drain/Still Pictures **page 20** The Edinburgh Photographic
Library **page 21** Dr Terry Jennings **page 22** (top) Skyscan
Photolibrary/Bob Evans (bottom) Skyscan Photolibrary/
Brian Lea **page 23** (left) Collections/Fay Godwin (right) Ken
Paterson ©/the Still Moving picture co **page 24** (top)
Quentin Bates/Ecoscene (bottom) Collections/Roger Scruton
page 25 (left) Ecoscene/Peter Hulme (right) © Doug
Allan/Oxford Scientific Films **page 26** Skyscan Photolibrary
page 27 (left) Collections/Roger Scruton (right)
Collections/Ed Gabriel **page 28** Rolf Richardson/Robert
Harding Picture Library **page 29** Skyscan Photolibrary
page 30 Skyscan Photolibrary **page 31** (top) Skyscan
Photolibrary (bottom) Collections/Kim Naylor **page 32**
Ecoscene **page 33** (top)Robert Harding Picture Library
(bottom) Robert Harding Picture Library/Adina Tovy **page
34** SkyscanPhotolibrary **page 35** (top) Robert Harding
Picture Library (bottom) HMS Customs and Excise **page 36**
Ecoscene/Ian Harwood **page 37** (top) © Jack Dermio/Oxford
Scientific Films (left) Chris Martin/Still Pictures (right)
Collections/Paul Watts **page 38** Dr Ben Hextall/Sylvia
Cordaiy Photo Library Ltd **page 39** (top) © Paul Kay/Oxford
Scientific Films (bottom) © Ben Osborne/Oxford Scientific
Films **page 40** (top) Dr Terry Jennings (bottom) Ecoscene/©
E J Bent **page 41** (left) Dr Terry Jennings (right) © Mark
Hamblin/Oxford Scientific Films **page 42** (top) © Jonathan
Smith/Sylvia Cordaiy Photo Library (bottom)
Collections/Paul Watts **page 43** Ecoscene/Ian Harwood

CONTENTS

WHERE THE LAND MEETS THE SEA

THE BRITISH ISLES CONSIST OF TWO LARGE ISLANDS, GREAT BRITAIN AND IRELAND, AND MORE THAN A THOUSAND SMALLER ISLANDS. THEY ARE SEPARATED FROM THE REST OF EUROPE BY THE ENGLISH CHANNEL AND THE NORTH SEA.

▲ The Giant's Causeway in Antrim Northern Ireland, was formed about 60 million years ago, when volcanic lava cooled rapidly.

◄ The huge blocks of rock at Bedruthan Steps in Cornwall are made of hard granite, but the softer rocks around them have been slowly eroded by the waves.

THE COASTLINE OF THE BRITISH ISLES, the place where the land meets the sea, is 14,000 kilometres long and one of the most varied and beautiful in the world. Towering cliffs, sandy beaches, long ridges of shingle, called spits, sand dunes and salt marshes all occur within a short distance of each other. The colours range from the dazzling white chalk cliffs of Dover and Beachy Head to the red sandstone of South Devon, and from the black basalt rock of the Giant's Causeway in Antrim, Northern Ireland, to the yellow and brown carboniferous limestone of the Cliffs of Moher in western Ireland and the grey gneiss rocks of the Outer Hebrides.

CHANGING COASTLINES

The coastline is always changing, shifting backwards, forwards and sideways as the forces of nature take over. The sea wears away, or erodes, the land in one location, carrying

▶ *Using the coast for holiday fun at Bournemouth on the south coast of England.*

away the mud, sand and shingle with the tides and depositing them elsewhere. Plants that are able to withstand the salt in the sea may colonise the mud, sand and shingle, gradually creating new land.

In the west of Britain and Ireland, the older, harder rocks that are fully exposed to westerly gales, form a rugged, irregular coastline. The east coast of Ireland is straighter, with many long, sandy beaches. The softer, more sheltered coastal areas of eastern and south-eastern England have large expanses of mud flats, salt marshes, sand dunes and crumbling cliffs that are formed from soil, clay, chalk or other soft rocks.

Our coastlines also change because of the actions of people. We alter the appearance of the coastline by building houses, shops, harbours, factories, power stations and amusement arcades along it. We change the shape of the coast by building sea walls, groynes and other sea defences. We remove sand, gravel and larger pieces of rock from the coast for building materials. We drill oil and gas for our fuel supplies. And we pollute the coast and sea with our waste, litter and sewage.

WILDLIFE AND THE COAST

Certain plants and animals can survive only on the coasts. Wild birds such as gulls, waders, cormorants, puffins, gannets and guillemots, and mammals such as the common seal and grey seal, visit the coast to feed, breed or simply to rest. Whales, porpoises and dolphins and many kinds of fish live and feed offshore.

In this book we look at some of the ways in which our coasts are being changed and how this affects important habitats for wildlife. We also examine how people use, and sometimes abuse, coastal areas. Finally, we consider the future prospects for our coasts.

THE MOVING SEA

THE CONSTANT MOVEMENT OF CURRENTS, TIDES AND WAVES
GRADUALLY ERODES THE COASTLINE, TRANSPORTING SMALL
PIECES OF ROCK FROM SHORE TO SHORE.

OCEAN CURRENTS

Currents are like giant rivers flowing across the oceans. Warm currents, driven by warm winds, flow across the surface of the ocean. Cold currents are produced deep in the ocean because cold water near the North and South Poles has sunk.

The main current that affects the British Isles is the Gulf Stream. It originates in the warm waters of the Caribbean and the Gulf of Mexico. Pushed along by the prevailing, or most common, south-westerly winds at an average speed of about 130 kilometres a day, the Gulf Stream then crosses the Atlantic Ocean towards Europe, where it becomes known as the North Atlantic Drift. This warm current helps to make the winters in the British Isles much milder than those of other places a similar distance north of the equator, such as Poland and Belarus.

OCEAN CURRENTS

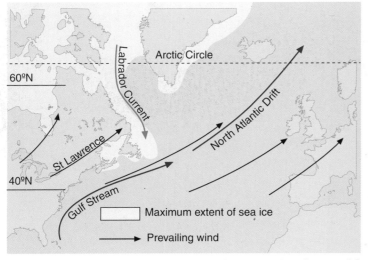

The map shows: Arctic Circle, 60°N, 40°N, Labrador Current, St Lawrence, Gulf Stream, North Atlantic Drift, Maximum extent of sea ice, Prevailing wind

▲ *The main currents affecting the British Isles. Cold currents are shown in blue and warm currents in red.*

TIDES

The level of the sea rises twice each day in most parts of the world, covering the seashore. People say the tide is 'in' or that it is 'high tide'. Twice a day the level of the sea falls and the tide goes 'out'. Then it is 'low tide'.

The tides are caused because the moon's pull, or gravity, causes the water in the oceans and seas to bulge out slightly on the part of Earth facing the moon. The oceans and seas directly opposite the moon also bulge out slightly. High tides are the two bulges and low tides are the hollows in between. As the Earth

▼ *It is easy to become stranded at high tide. This air-sea rescue helicopter is demonstrating how to rescue someone trapped on the cliffs.*

THE SEVERN 'BORE'

The tidal range in the funnel-shaped estuary of the River Severn is the highest in the British Isles at 12.4 metres. At certain times, when the incoming high tide of the sea meets the outgoing river water, a giant moving wave that may be more than two metres high, is created. This 'bore', as it is called, rushes up the river, sometimes flooding its banks.

---

turns on its axis each day, places move in and out of these bulges causing their sea levels to rise and fall.

The sun's gravity also pulls on the oceans and seas. Twice each month the sun, moon and Earth are in a line. When the pull of the sun is added to that of the moon, it makes the rise and fall of the sea even more pronounced. These 'extra' high tides are called 'spring tides'.

Although the force of gravity of the moon and sun are the same all over the Earth, the difference in the level of the water between the highest and lowest tides varies greatly from place to place. Over the open Atlantic Ocean this tidal range, as it is called, is generally less than one metre. Around the coasts of the British Isles the tidal range is frequently more than five metres. It is greatest in shallow estuaries. In the port of Liverpool, for example, there is a tidal range during spring tides of as much as ten metres. Southampton Water, between the Isle of Wight and the mainland, is unique in that there are four high tides every 24 hours instead of the usual one.

HOW A WAVE IS FORMED

Direction of wind →

crest

crest

trough

trough

wave breaks

water moves in a circle

WAVES AND STORM SURGES

Waves are made by the wind blowing across the water. They vary in size from small ripples to gigantic, crashing breakers that pound the shore. In the open sea, waves look as if they are moving forwards, but they are, in fact, moving in a circle. The hollow between two waves is called a 'trough'. The harder the wind blows, the bigger the waves and the deeper the troughs in between them. Near the shore, some of the moving water drags across the sea bed, slowing each wave. Then the crest of the wave curves over, or 'breaks'.

When the wind and tides combine, they produce what is called a 'storm surge' of waves that can be over three metres high. A storm surge can cause widespread flooding in low-lying areas, as occurred in the North Sea in 1953. A surge swamped the east coast of England and the Thames estuary, flooding London. Over 300 people died.

▲ *The huge, crashing waves near the Cliffs of Moher in Ireland are created by the strong wind blowing towards the land.*

EROSION

WHERE HIGH GROUND MEETS THE SEA, THERE ARE STEEP ROCK FACES, OR CLIFFS. CLIFFS ARE CONSTANTLY UNDER ATTACK BY THE SEA, SLOWLY RETREATING INLAND DUE TO THE PROCESS OF EROSION.

CONSTANT POUNDING by the waves at the bottom of the cliffs takes its toll. Gradually a hollow forms. If the waves are carrying pebbles and other rock fragments picked up from the shore, the base of the cliff erodes even faster. Eventually the rocks above collapse. The erosion continues until a flat area of rock, called a wave-cut platform, remains, marking the place where the cliff once stood.

Cliffs are eroded by two other methods. As a wave breaks against the cliff, it forces air into cracks and crevices and compresses it. When the water retreats, the compressed air expands with such an explosive force that it weakens even the toughest rock. Another method of erosion is caused by the acid in sea water dissolving certain rocks, particularly chalk or limestone.

When cliffs are made of soil or soft rocks – such as clay, chalk and some sandstones, as along much of the coast of eastern England – they erode quickly. The western coasts of the British Isles are made of much tougher rocks, such as granite, carboniferous limestone and hard sandstone, and they erode much more slowly. The low clay cliffs near Holderness in East Yorkshire are eroding at the rate of about two metres a year. Since Roman times, this coastline has been pushed back a distance of four kilometres and at least 36 villages have been lost to the sea. Dunwich in Suffolk, also on the east coast of England, was once a large and prosperous port. But in 1326 a savage storm swept away three of the town's nine churches and 400 houses. Since then, more and more of the town has slipped into the sea as the soft, sandy cliffs have been eroded by the waves. The last of the original churches fell into the sea in 1919. Now just a few houses remain in Dunwich and a more modern church.

◀ *This flat, limestone wave-cut platform in Glamorgan, South Wales, has been created by erosion of the cliffs.*

◀ *The erosion of the soft cliffs at Scarborough in Yorkshire caused a landslide, in June 1993, in which a large hotel fell into the sea.*

THE HIGHEST CLIFFS
● The highest cliffs in the British Isles, at 400 metres, are the Conachair cliffs on the island of St Kilda in the Western Isles.
● The highest sheer sea cliffs on the mainland of Great Britain are at Clo Mor, near the northern tip of Scotland. They drop 281 metres to the sea.

▼ *The soft, chalk cliffs of the Old Harry Rocks in Dorset have been worn away, leaving two arches and stacks.*

BAYS, HEADLANDS AND CAVES

When a cliff is made of both hard rocks, such as granite or limestone, and soft rocks, such as chalk, clay or sand, the soft rocks are the first to erode, forming bays. The hard rocks stand alone, jutting out as headlands.

Sometimes the waves slowly cut a hollow into a cliff, forming a cave.

Once a cave has been made, the waves may then punch a hole, called a blowhole, through its roof. If caves form on opposite sides of a headland, they could eventually meet to form an arch. If the roof of the arch falls in, it leaves a column of rock called a stack. In time the stack will completely erode away too.

▶ *The bay of Lulworth Cove in Dorset.*

BEACHES AND DUNES

THE SEA EVENTUALLY DEPOSITS THE MATERIAL ERODED FROM CLIFFS AND OTHER PARTS OF THE COAST. AFTER MANY, SOMETIMES HUNDREDS OF YEARS, THIS MATERIAL CAN FORM NEW LAND.

BEACHES ARE STRIPS of land at the edge of the sea, made up from boulders, pebbles and sand washed up by the sea.

When waves wear away cliffs, arches and stacks, large pieces of rock, or boulders, break off and crash down to the beach below. There they are broken down by the waves into smaller and smaller pieces. The corners of each piece of rock are knocked off and smoothed down by other pieces of rock and by the action of the sea. Even man-made materials, such as brick, concrete and glass, become pebble-shaped after being in the sea for some time. The pebbles are swept along by tides and currents, grinding together until eventually they become sand.

PEBBLY AND SANDY BEACHES

In open, windy places, where powerful waves roll in, beaches are usually made up of pebbles. The waves have the energy to throw the pebbles on to the beach, but there is not enough power in the backwash of the waves to sweep the pebbles back out to sea.

At the back of some beaches, particularly those that face the open Atlantic Ocean, large boulders are often found. This type of beach is called a 'storm beach'. The boulders have been thrown up by the waves during storms.

Some of the sand on beaches comes from local cliffs. Sand sometimes contains crushed-up seashells – the remains of shellfish such as cockles and razorfish that live in the sand close to the low-tide mark. Over thousands of years, huge quantities of empty shells are sometimes thrown up on to the shore, creating a new beach. There is a 'shell beach' on the island of Herm in the Channel Islands and another at Mochras in Harlech, Wales. At Connemara in western Ireland, one beach

▲ *A storm beach in County Kerry, Ireland.*
▶ *Further down, the beach is sandy. Boulders that have fallen from the cliffs have been slowly ground together by the action of the waves, creating sand.*

◄ *Sand dunes and the long sandy beach at Bamburgh Castle in Northumberland.*

▶ *Sand dunes are fragile. The plants that hold them together are damaged when people walk on them.*

looks white because it is built up from the minute shells of deep-sea animals called foraminifera.

Most of the sand on beaches, however, has been brought down to the sea by rivers. The rocks the rivers carry are worn away until silt and sand are formed. The tiniest particles of clay and silt are carried far out to sea, but the larger, heavier grains of sand settle near the shore, often far from the mouth of the river. The sand only settles where the waves are gentle, for example in a bay or cove that is sheltered from strong winds.

SAND DUNES

Often the wind redistributes the sand on beaches. When wet sand dries out, even gentle breezes can lift up some of the grains. If the grains are blown inland, they collect behind any form of shelter, including stones, pieces of wood and even old shoes! Eventually the sand piles up into hills called sand dunes. The dunes at Culbin Sands on the east coast of

Scotland – the largest in the British Isles – reach heights of 30 metres.

In time, perhaps over hundreds of years, the wind can push the dune inland, burying forests and buildings. Usually, however, certain grasses, particularly marram grass, begin to grow on the dune. Marram grass is unusual because it can withstand being buried under salty sand. Its network of roots help to hold the sand dune in place, whilst its leaves shelter the surface of the sand from the wind. If left undisturbed, the marram grass can stabilise the dune, allowing other plants to grow on it. Eventually a row of dunes can form new land. Many areas on the coast that were once sand dunes are now used as golf courses.

In spite of their size, sand dunes are fragile. A break in the thin covering of plants – caused by fire or by people walking or playing on them – gives the wind the chance to resume its attack. A huge hole or 'blow-out' is made in the dunes, which may take many years to re-form. The blow-out may even allow the sea to flood the land beyond the dunes.

NEW BEACHES FROM OLD

SOME OF OUR BEACHES ARE DISAPPEARING. OTHERS ARE BEING CREATED AS SAND AND PEBBLES WASHED UP BY THE WAVES CREATE NEW COASTAL SCENERY.

THE FORCE THAT drives the waves is the wind. For a particular beach, however, there is usually one direction from which waves approach most often or with greatest force. But when the waves break, the water goes straight back down the beach, creating a zigzag pattern on the shore. Any sand or pebbles carried by the waves also travel along the beach in the same way.

LONGSHORE DRIFT

The zigzag movement of material along the shore is called longshore drift. Longshore drift can carry sand and pebbles great distances. In southern England, for example, unusual pebbles from the coast at Budleigh Salterton in south Devon have been discovered on beaches in Kent and Sussex, more than 300 kilometres further east.

▲ *Sometimes it is necessary to replace or redistribute the sand or pebbles that have been washed away by longshore drift.*

Longshore drift can cause serious problems. Entire beaches can be carried away and deposited elsewhere. Some holiday resorts have to bring in sand to replenish their eroded beaches. The sand and pebbles dumped by the sea can also block harbours, ruining the business of the ports. Cley and Blakeney in Norfolk, Rye in Sussex, Alnmouth in Northumberland and Wexford in Ireland are just a few of the ports that have been affected by longshore drift in the past, before efficient, yet expensive, dredging

LONGSHORE DRIFT

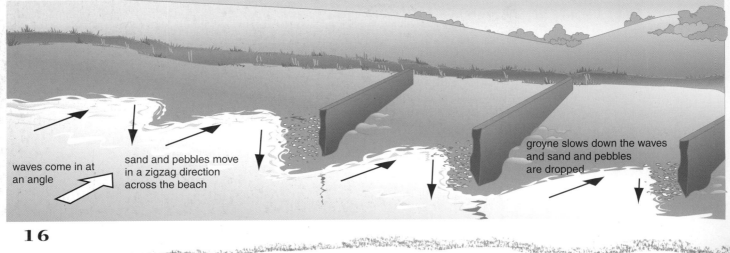

waves come in at an angle

sand and pebbles move in a zigzag direction across the beach

groyne slows down the waves and sand and pebbles are dropped

equipment became available. These ports are now used only by small boats.

SPITS, BARS AND LAGOONS

The sand and pebbles carried by longshore drift may eventually be dropped when the angle of the shore changes, thus slowing the flow of water. This usually happens in a bay or at the mouth of a river, where the sea is deeper. The waves slow down and drop the materials they are carrying.

After many, sometimes hundreds, of years, the sand and pebbles pile so high that they form a ridge across the bay or river mouth, known as a spit. Spurn Head on the Humber estuary is one example. There are many other famous spits, including those at Dawlish Warren in Devon, Hurst Spit in Hampshire

and Orfordness in Suffolk. If a spit extends across the bay or river mouth, it is called a bar, and the shallow pool of water trapped behind the bar is known as a lagoon. The longest bar in Europe is Chesil Beach in Dorset. It is sixteen kilometres long and encloses a lagoon known as the Fleet.

If a spit builds up across the mouth of a river, it can force the river to find a new outlet to the sea. This happened at the estuary of Afon Mawddach in West Wales, while the town of Great Yarmouth in Norfolk is actually built on a spit that caused the local river, the River Yare, to change its course.

▼ *An aerial photograph of Chesil Beach in Dorset, the longest bar in the British Isles. This shingle bank, 16 kilometres long and between 180 and 900 metres wide, separates the sea from a lagoon.*

▲ *Spurn Head, at the mouth of the Humber estuary, is an example of a spit. It is made from sand and shingle and is about 5.5 kilometres long but, in places, only about 50 metres wide.*

PROTECTING THE COASTLINE

ALONG SOME PARTS OF THE COAST, LAND IS BEING ERODED AT THE RATE OF MORE THAN ONE METRE A YEAR. THIS RATE OF EROSION IS INCREASING AS SEA LEVELS RISE DUE TO GLOBAL WARMING. EFFECTIVE METHODS OF HOLDING BACK THE SEA ARE VITAL.

▲ The breakwaters at the entrance to the harbour at Whitby in North Yorkshire help to shelter the boats in the harbour from the force of the waves during stormy weather.

SEA WALLS BUILT of stone or concrete protect beaches and buildings near the sea. Most modern sea walls are curved so that they push the waves upwards and back out to sea again. They are very expensive. A sea wall that is three metres high costs £400,000 per kilometre, and one twelve metres high costs £5 million per kilometre. The disadvantages of building sea walls are that they can look unsightly and they can damage marshes and other wildlife habitats by depriving them of sea water.

Breakwaters are long barriers of boulders or concrete that extend into the sea. They are used to protect harbours during stormy weather. However, they can simply redirect the damaging effects of the waves to another location along the coast.

Groynes are fences that are built on beaches at right angles to the sea. They slow down the

◄ Repairing the groynes on the beach at Eastbourne in East Sussex. Because they are usually made of wood, groynes eventually rot and have to be replaced.

DISAPPEARING COASTLINE

- The longest breakwater in the British Isles is at Holyhead in Anglesey, North Wales. It was completed in 1873 and is 2394 metres long - the length of over 20 football pitches.
- The Holderness coastline in East Yorkshire is eroding at an average rate of 2 metres a year.
- English Nature, a government environmental organisation, estimates that at least 13,000 hectares of English coastline will disappear into the sea in the next 20 years.

water currents, preventing sand and pebbles from being washed away by longshore drift.

In some places on the east coast of England, artificial reefs – long rows of rocks or boulders built up from the sea bed and running parallel to the coastline – are being built to reduce the power of the waves.

'SOFT ENGINEERING'

Sand dunes are fragile and easily damaged. When the wind blows hard, dunes can be blown away, allowing the sea to flood inland. To prevent this, people plant grasses, such as marram grass, and even pine trees to help hold the dunes in place.

Increasingly people are being encouraged to use similar 'soft engineering' methods for protecting the coast, instead of the more expensive methods ('hard engineering') of building sea walls, breakwaters, groynes and reefs. Improved drainage of cliffs, for example, can help to prevent cliff falls. In January 1999, thousands of tonnes of chalk crashed from the top of Beachy Head in East Sussex to the beach below. The fall was probably caused by heavy rain and could have been prevented had the cliffs been better drained – a relatively easy and inexpensive thing to do.

Sometimes 'managed retreat' is the best way to protect the coast. A few years ago, the Environment Agency decided not to spend £500,000 on building a sea wall at Orplands in Essex to defend 100 hectares of farmland. Instead the area was allowed to flood, so that it became a salt marsh – a rich habitat for wading birds, wildfowl, salt marsh plants and other wildlife. Just as importantly, the marsh breaks the force of the waves, preventing flooding further inland.

▼ Planting marram grass on the dunes in South Wales helps to repair past damage.

CHANGING SEA LEVELS

THE LEVEL OF THE SEA AROUND THE BRITISH ISLES HAS NOT ALWAYS
BEEN THE SAME AS IT IS NOW. IN SOME PLACES, THE SEA LEVEL HAS
RISEN, AND IN OTHERS, THE LAND HAS BEEN FORCED UPWARDS.

OVER THE LAST 18,000 years, the sea level has risen by about 120 metres. At the end of the Ice Age, the ice and snow that covered much of the land started to melt. Many low-lying coastal areas were flooded as the sea flowed inland. Until about 12,000 years ago, the land now known as the British Isles was joined to mainland Europe. As the sea level rose at the end of the Ice Age, the British Isles was isolated as water poured through what we now call the Straits of Dover and the Irish Sea. On several beaches in West Wales, North Norfolk, Bexhill in Sussex and at Bridgwater Bay in Somerset, it is possible, at low tide, to see the remains of forests that were flooded and destroyed when the sea level rose.

SEA LOCHS, FJORDS AND RIAS

During the Ice Age, glaciers carved out deep U-shaped valleys as they moved towards the sea. When the sea level rose, the valleys were flooded, creating long stretches of water with steep sides. The sea lochs of Western Scotland and the fjords of the Shetland Isles and Norway were formed in this way.

Many river valleys were flooded at the same time. The submerged river valleys became long, winding inlets, called rias. The deep inlets of the Severn estuary in England, the Firth of Forth in Scotland, and Dingle Bay and Bantry Bay in south-west Ireland are rias. A ria is often used as a site for a port, because it

THE BRITISH ISLES DURING THE LAST ICE AGE

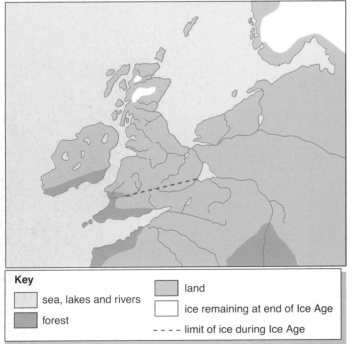

Key

▨ sea, lakes and rivers

▨ forest

▨ land

☐ ice remaining at end of Ice Age

- - - - limit of ice during Ice Age

During the Ice Age the British Isles was joined to Europe. Only when the ice melted did they separate.

▲ *Loch Linnhe in western Scotland is a sea loch that was formed by glaciers during the Ice Age. It was then flooded when the ice melted and the sea level rose.*

provides an area of deep water sheltered from the waves of the sea. The ria of Milford Haven is used as a fishing port and is the site of one of the largest oil ports in Europe.

RAISED BEACHES

In some places on the coast, the land has been forced upwards. It took 6000 years for the ice to melt from the British Isles at the end of the last Ice Age. As it melted, the weight of the ice on the land decreased and so the land slowly began to rise – rather like a spring mattress. Parts of the sea bed became land. This process is still going on, and in certain locations beaches and cliffs have been pushed above the sea level. The beaches are known as raised beaches and there are many examples on the west coast of Scotland and the Western Isles, in South Wales and along the coast of Devon.

▼ *This raised beach is near Prawle Point in south Devon. The flat, grassy area near the sea is the old beach and the steeper ground to the left is the old cliff line.*

GLOBAL WARMING

World average temperatures are rising because of global warming, and the ice caps around the North and South Poles are starting to melt. Sea levels across the world have risen by between 10 and 25 centimetres over the last century. Scientists believe that this is due partly to the melting of the ice caps and partly to the increase in temperatures which have caused the water in the oceans and seas to expand slightly. It is estimated that by the year 2030 sea levels in south-east England will have risen by 20 centimetres, flooding many low-lying areas.

GLOBAL WARMING
- The amount of carbon dioxide gas in the air has risen by 30 per cent since the end of the last Ice Age, mainly due to the burning of coal, oil, gas and forests.
- The average air temperature has risen by 0.3°C to 0.6°C since the mid-nineteenth century. In the Antarctic, however, average temperatures have risen by around 2.5°C since the 1940s when records were first kept.

ISLANDS

MORE THAN A THOUSAND ISLANDS, RANGING FROM SMALL UNINHABITED LUMPS OF ROCK TO THE LARGE ISLAND OF GREAT BRITAIN, MAKE UP THE BRITISH ISLES, WHICH HAS A POPULATION OF OVER 62 MILLION.

▲ *The Farne Islands are an island archipelago between 2.5 and 7 kilometres from the mainland of Northumberland. These rocky islands are an important nesting site for sea birds and one of the main breeding grounds of the grey seal.*

ISLANDS ARE PIECES OF LAND surrounded by water. The western and northern coastlines of Britain and Ireland, which were flooded at the end of the Ice Age, are dotted with small islands. There are, for example, more than 100 small islands in Clew Bay on the west coast of Ireland. By contrast, apart from the Isle of Wight, no large island lies off the southern or eastern coasts. Most of the rocks along the south and east coasts are soft clays, sandstones and chalks, and any islands formed quickly wear away. Although the Isle of Wight is made mainly of soft chalk and sandstone, it is large and sheltered by the mainland from which it was cut off thousands of years ago.

The islands around Great Britain and Ireland are all fairly close to the mainland and are consequently made of rocks very similar to those of the mainland. The Isles of Scilly, for example, are made of the same granite rock that forms Lands End.

Most of the islands around the British Isles were separated from the mainland by rising sea levels after the last Ice Age. In some places the sea cut through a narrow peninsula of rock, leaving an isolated headland. In other places, dry land sank into the sea, leaving only the tops of mountains above the water, which formed a group of islands called an archipelago.

▼ *St Michael's Mount in Cornwall shows how an island is formed. It is cut off from the mainland only at high tide.*

◀ *A farmer transports sheep to summer pasture in the Shetland Isles.*
▼ *A weaver in the Western Isles makes the famous hard-wearing woollen cloth known as Harris tweed.*

ISLAND LIFE

Because they are cut off from the mainland, islanders rely on fishing and farming to make their living, as they have done for years. Fishermen and farmers have occupied the three Aran islands, off the west coast of Ireland, since prehistoric times. The early inhabitants laid seaweed and sand on bare rock to make fields on which to grow potatoes and other crops and they protected them with high stone walls. But a new industry has emerged in recent years – tourism. Over 200,000 tourists arrive every year.

The Shetland Islands are an archipelago of more than 100 islands off north-east Scotland. Only fifteen of the islands are inhabited, even though some of them are quite large. Most Shetlanders earned a living by fishing and sheep-farming until the discovery of North Sea oil. Now the oil industry is one of the main employers. Tourism is another. The population of the Islands has increased from 20,000 in 1975 to more than 28,000 today because of these industries.

The people who live on small islands can often feel lonely and isolated from modern-day life. Usually there are few opportunities for skilled work, and so the younger, more active inhabitants leave to find work on the mainland. Left behind are the elderly, the unskilled and those working in farming and fishing. Some of the smaller islands have lost their communities. The last 30 residents left the island of St Kilda in 1930. The island of Scarp, off north-west Scotland, had a population of 50 in 1965 and its own school. But all the inhabitants have now left.

THE LARGEST ISLANDS
- Great Britain is the eighth largest island in the world, with an area of almost 230,000 sq km.
- Although Australia is sometimes called an island continent, Greenland is generally considered to be the largest island in the world, with an area of about 2,175,600 square kilometres. The other large islands, in order of size, are: New Guinea, Borneo, Madagascar, Baffin, Sumatra, Honshu and Great Britain.

FOOD FROM THE SEA

THE COMBINATION OF SHALLOW
SEAS AND THE MIXING OF WATERS
BY CURRENTS PROVIDES
A RICH FOOD SOURCE FOR
FISH AND SHELLFISH.

▲ *Fishermen sorting the catch on the deck of a deep-sea trawler.*

▶ *Whitby was once a whaling port. As whaling declined, it turned to herrings, which are now also scarce.*

THERE ARE TWO main groups of fish around the coasts of the British Isles – fish such as cod, haddock, sole and plaice that live near the sea bed and fish such as herring and mackerel that live near the surface of the water. Different methods are used to catch them. Lobsters, crabs, cockles, mussels, shrimps and prawns are found in estuaries and in the sea just off the coasts.

Almost every coastal village has some fishermen who provide fish for the local population. Lobsters and crabs are caught in baited traps set close to the shore, and the smaller fishing boats also tend to fish close to the coast. The fishermen use lines with hooks, or small nets.

Larger trawlers go further afield, and the possibility of deep-sea fishing trips lasting three or four weeks have become possible because the ships are equipped with modern navigational equipment and methods of freezing the catch.

OVERFISHING

There has been a dramatic decline in the British fishing industry in recent years. Even so, there are still 18,600 fishermen in the United Kingdom and 6000 in Ireland, with more people employed in processing and distribution.

One reason for the decrease in sea fishing is that most countries have established a 200-mile (320 km) fishing limit around their coasts and only a small number of foreign fishing vessels are allowed within that zone. British ships can no longer fish the distant fishing grounds off Iceland, Greenland and Canada as they once did.

If managed properly, fishing is a sustainable activity that can go on providing fish. But the British Isles' fishing industry, as throughout the rest of the world, has declined because of 'overfishing'. It has become more mechanised and many ships fish the same waters with huge nets that do not allow the younger fish to escape and breed. This type of fishing is not sustainable, and in order to try and increase stocks there are now restrictions on when and how many fish can be caught.

GENETIC MODIFICATION

Scientists can now create plants and animals that nature itself has never created by changing, or modifying, the genes within existing plants and animals. Genes determine how living things develop and function. Salmon and trout can now grow four times faster and larger because of an added growth hormone. So far, public opposition has prevented these 'genetically modified' fish from being farmed on a large scale.

FISH FARMING

In some sheltered bays, estuaries and sea lochs, fish and shellfish such as crabs, lobsters, oysters, mussels, prawns, salmon, trout, plaice and sole are now being 'farmed'. In Ireland, experiments are taking place to try to farm certain kinds of seaweed for human consumption. Fish farming is possible only where the sea water is clean and unpolluted, in order to keep the fish healthy. The droppings from so many fish and the collection of stale, uneaten food in a small area breed germs. Medicines and chemicals are used to keep the farmed fish healthy, but these substances also pollute the water.

◀ *Feeding time at a salmon fish farm in the Shetland Islands. Fish farming is only possible where the water is clean and unpolluted.*

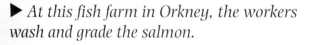

▶ *At this fish farm in Orkney, the workers wash and grade the salmon.*

ENERGY AND MINERALS FROM THE SEA

WIND, WAVE AND TIDAL POWER PROVIDE US WITH SUSTAINABLE FORMS OF ENERGY.

GAS AND OIL

Oil is one of the most important substances in the world today. It provides fuel for motor vehicles and power stations and it is used in the manufacture of plastics, chemicals and many clothes.

Both oil and gas are found under the sea bed. Once an oil or gas field has been discovered, a drilling rig is erected and the drilling begins. The oil is usually transported from the rig to the refineries by pipeline, but over long distances tankers are used. The gas is piped ashore. The first oil wells were drilled in the bed of the North Sea in 1965. By 1997 there were 186 offshore oil and gas fields in operation in the North Sea. There is also a gas field in Morecambe Bay and two more off the south coast of Ireland, but because the Irish fields are running out, a gas pipeline is being built from Scotland to Ireland to boost supplies.

The supplies of oil and gas around our shores will not last forever. It is estimated that oil will run out in the next 40 years and natural gas in 60 years if we go on using them at the present rate. There will then be the problem of safely sealing off the old wells and disposing of the unwanted drilling platforms without harming the environment.

POWER STATIONS

Most of our electricity is produced in power stations. There are about 150 sited on or near the coasts of the British Isles. The amount of water they use can have serious effects on local marine life.

▶ *The nuclear power station at Hinckley Point on the Bristol Channel coast of Somerset. Power stations use huge quantities of water for cooling purposes, and return it, at a much higher temperature, to the sea. Power stations also pump some of their waste into the sea. The warm water can harm fish and other sea creatures as it contains less oxygen.*

◀ *Wind turbines at Blyth, Northumberland. Although they can be noisy, the turbines produce electricity without polluting the air, water or soil.*

▼ *The tidal mill at Woodbridge, Suffolk was powered by the ebb and flow of the tides. It could work for only two hours before low tide and two hours afterwards.*

WIND AND WATER POWER

Wind power has been used for centuries. Old windmills can still be seen near our coasts, as well as a few old tidal mills, which used the energy of the tides to grind corn and turn machinery. The best-known mills are at Woodbridge in Suffolk and Eling in Hampshire. Unlike coal, oil, gas, or nuclear power, the energy produced by the wind and tides will not run out and it does not pollute the environment. There are modern wind turbines that produce electricity on or near our coasts, and the building of many more is planned. Although there is a power station on the estuary of the River Rance in northern France that uses the energy of the tides to produce electricity, so far there are no plans for similar power stations to be built in the British Isles. However, scientists in Ireland are developing a machine that uses wave power to produce electricity.

SAND AND GRAVEL

The demand for sand and gravel for building, or for replenishing beaches, is also increasing. Most of it comes from quarries on land, but about four per cent comes from the sea bed. Although there appears to be plenty of sand and gravel around our coasts, at the present rate of use supplies will be exhausted within the next 15 to 20 years. Obtaining sand and gravel from the sea bed destroys the habitats of sea animals and plants, smothers fish eggs and shellfish and, by lowering the level of the sea bed, increases erosion of the shore.

WIND TURBINES
- There are 55 sites using wind turbines in the United Kingdom. They produce enough electricity for over 250,000 homes.
- The largest wind turbine in the United Kingdom is at the Ecotech Centre at Swaffham in Norfolk. The tower is 67 metres high – taller than the Statue of Liberty; the height of the turbine from the top of the propeller blade to the bottom of the tower is 100 metres. The Ecotech wind turbine produces enough electricity to power 15,000 television sets.

COASTAL FORTIFICATIONS

THE PEOPLE OF THE BRITISH ISLES HAVE ALWAYS HAD TO
DEFEND THEMSELVES FROM ATTACKS BY RAIDERS FROM
OVERSEAS. THEY BUILT CASTLES AND OTHER
FORTIFICATIONS FOR THEIR OWN PROTECTION.

AT THE END OF THE third century AD, when the Romans occupied Britain, the Saxons crossed the North Sea and the eastern English Channel to launch their attacks. To fend them off the Romans built a series of forts around the eastern and southern coasts of England. Examples still remain at Burgh Castle in Norfolk, Richborough in Kent and Porchester in Hampshire.

The Vikings, from Norway, Denmark and Sweden, first invaded the British Isles in the eighth century, when they established themselves in the Shetland and Orkney Islands. Later, they settled in parts of England and on the east coast of Ireland. The only English kingdom to resist them was Wessex, ruled by King Alfred. He had built a chain of castles, called burhs, along the coast and borders of his kingdom. Some of these burhs later developed into towns, such as Chichester in Sussex and Wareham in Dorset.

THE FIRST CASTLES

The first castles were built in tenth-century France. During the eleventh century they became popular all over Western Europe. Originally the castles were the private fortresses of kings or noblemen and their families, servants and workers. Castles such as Deal and Walmer in Kent and Pendennis and St Mawes in Cornwall were built in medieval times as part of a national policy to protect the British against foreign invasion and coastal raiding, mainly from France.

The threat of invasion from France by Napoleon's armies between 1804 and 1812

▲ *Carrickfergus was probably the first stone castle to be built in Ireland. The great tower was started in the 1190s. It was besieged and damaged at least twice in the Middle Ages.*

led to the construction of a chain of circular towers – Martello towers – along the south and east coast of England. One hundred and three were built and 45 still remain.

▲ *The restored Martello tower at Dymchurch, Kent.*

MODERN WARFARE

During the two World Wars, the British Isles again faced the threat of attack, this time from both the sea and the air. At first people relied on the Royal Navy to protect them from invasion. However, the German naval bombardment of Hartlepool and Scarborough in 1914 and the rapid advance of the German armies towards the coast of Belgium raised fears of an invasion. Defences, especially on the east and south-east coasts were strengthened, a process that continued during the Second World War. Pillboxes, tank traps and the remains of airfields and radar stations built to defend Britain and to carry out bombing raids on German-occupied Europe can still be seen along the south and east coasts. Many airfields later became farms, and some became civilian airports.

COASTAL TOWNS AND CITIES

MANY OF THE LARGEST TOWNS AND CITIES IN THE BRITISH ISLES ARE ON OR NEAR THE COAST, INCLUDING THE CAPITAL CITIES OF LONDON, DUBLIN, EDINBURGH, CARDIFF AND BELFAST.

THERE ARE MANY REASONS why towns and cities exist where they do today. Originally people built their homes close together for protection, companionship and safety. The first settlers had to make sure that the area they lived in could provide food, water, materials for making their homes and clothes, and fuel for fires and cooking.

As time passes, settlements change, and over a long period of time many villages grew into towns. The town of South Shields on the southern bank of the River Tyne was once a Roman fort. Scarborough was once a village with a medieval castle built on a rocky headland of the coast.

Villages often developed where there were rich fishing grounds and sheltered harbours. Kingston-upon-Hull, Grimsby, Great Yarmouth, Lowestoft, Brixham, Milford Haven, Fraserburgh, Sligo and Dingle are a few such examples.

Settlements that could be reached by large ships became ports. London, Bristol, Glasgow, Belfast, Cork and Dublin all developed on such sites, while Newcastle developed on the site where the major road from London to Edinburgh crossed the River Tyne.

Other towns and cities grew because there were important resources and industries in the area. The towns of Amble and Blyth in north-east England were close to major coalfields and so they started to export coal. Before the Industrial Revolution, Swansea was a small harbour and fishing village. The plentiful supply of coal and copper ore nearby led to the building of smelting works to make copper. The harbour expanded and, by the middle of the nineteenth century, more than 10,000 ships were sailing in and out of the port each year.

THE GROWTH OF RESORTS

Fine, wide sandy beaches are popular with tourists, which is why resorts such as Bournemouth, Bridlington, Skegness, Hunstanton, Southend, Torquay, St. Andrews, Llandudno and Ballycastle have developed. Many people, having spent happy holidays at a seaside resort, decide to retire there, which increases the local population. Coastal towns such as Bournemouth, Brighton, Bognor

◀ *The Marina in the centre of Kingston-upon-Hull was once the entrance to the fishing docks, which have now been redeveloped.*

◀ *Many of the old dockside buildings in Liverpool have been converted into museums, art galleries, television studios, shops, flats and offices.*

▼ *In spite of its shingle beach, Brighton is still popular with holidaymakers.*

Regis and Eastbourne have a high percentage of retired people. And resorts within easy travelling distance of large cities often grow because people who work in the cities prefer to spend their weekends and leisure time by the sea.

THE STORY OF LIVERPOOL

In the seventeenth century, Liverpool was a small fishing village. Liverpool began to grow in the late seventeenth and eighteenth centuries because of trade with America and Africa, first in slaves and sugar, and then in cotton. In the nineteenth century, Liverpool was one of the biggest and most prosperous ports in the world; it became the main port for people migrating from Britain to the United States. By 1880, docks stretched for twelve kilometres along the banks of the Mersey and 40 per cent of the world's trade was carried in Liverpool ships. Meanwhile, on the south shore, Birkenhead grew to provide more docks and shipbuilding yards. Eventually, Liverpool and Birkenhead were linked by road tunnels.

Today, much of the original dockland area is no longer used for cargo-handling because container ships and bulk carriers are now used. The thousands of passengers who travelled to and from America by sea now go by air. Many of the dockside warehouses and other buildings have been demolished or converted into museums, art galleries, television studios, shops, restaurants, flats and offices. Today the port still handles similar volumes of cargo to the 1950s and 1960s, but from new docks nearer the mouth of the estuary. The population of that once small village of Liverpool is now nearly half a million.

TOURISM AND LEISURE

MOST PEOPLE VISIT THE COAST TO BATHE, SUNBATHE, AND TO ENJOY THE FRESH SEA AIR AND COASTAL SCENERY. BUT GOING TO THE COAST FOR PLEASURE IS A RELATIVELY NEW IDEA.

▶ *Donkey rides are still a popular activity on the sands at Blackpool.*

BRIGHTON FOR HEALTH

Originally a small fishing port, Brighton was the first seaside resort in the British Isles. In 1750, Dr Richard Russell wrote a book claiming that bathing in the sea and drinking sea water at Brighton was a cure for certain diseases. Dr Russell's treatment proved very popular with the wealthy, including the Prince of Wales, who liked Brighton so much he went to live there.

In those days it was difficult to reach Brighton from London even though it was only 75 kilometres away. The journey took about seven hours along bumpy roads. But the coming of the railway in 1841 allowed thousands of day-trippers to visit Brighton because the journey time was reduced to 100 minutes. With the invention of coaches and cars and the growth of annual holidays, Brighton soon became known as 'London-by-the-Sea'. Other seaside resorts developed for similar reasons, and by the early years of the 20th century, millions of day-trippers and holiday-makers were visiting the coast from the industrial towns and cities inland. Other people moved to seaside resorts to retire.

RESORTS FOR ALL

Today the attractions of a seaside resort are many and varied. Apart from the sea, beach and coastal scenery, there are hotels, guesthouses, camping sites, amusement arcades, funfairs, marinas and some pleasure piers. Restaurants, cafés, theatres, cinemas and nightclubs cater for the visitors. Some beaches are protected by lifeguards, perhaps with a lifeboat station too, thereby providing tourists with a relatively safe environment.

A successful visit to the seaside usually depends on good weather, and a bad summer can have a disastrous effect on the income of businesses in resorts. There can also be high unemployment in the winter. In recent years, there has been a decline in the number of people taking their annual holiday in the British Isles because of the growth of cheaper 'package' holidays overseas. To counteract this trend, most resorts now try to attract visitors for weekends and short breaks. Also, some larger resorts have built conference centres to stimulate business throughout the year, while others are putting some of their attractions undercover so that they can be used all year.

▲ *The railway first brought crowds of people to Llandudno in the nineteenth century. Today it is still a popular resort and conference centre.*

LLANDUDNO

Llandudno, with its two long sandy beaches on either side of a towering limestone headland, the Great Orme, is one of the major holiday resorts in Wales. Like many resorts, Llandudno has a pier on which there are amusements and attractions for visitors. But to increase its year-round trade, the resort has built a large conference centre, an undercover shopping area and a 1500-seat theatre, as well as art galleries, museums, golf clubs and swimming baths.

CULTURAL AND HERITAGE TOURISM

Some resorts are using their links with the arts to appeal to tourists. South Shields, for example, promotes its association with the author Catherine Cookson, while Great Yarmouth describes how it is featured in the works of Charles Dickens. The real Alice in Wonderland, Alice Liddell, spent her childhood summers in Llandudno and the resort has built an Alice in Wonderland Centre. Other resorts featured in films or television dramas are quick to promote the fact in their marketing campaigns.

PROBLEMS

Unfortunately, a constant flow of visitors can harm coastal attractions. Many seaside resorts have narrow streets, which were never built for heavy motor traffic, and noise and litter can be a problem. Some developments, such as caravan sites and theme parks, change the coastal scenery and affect the habitats of coastal wildlife.

▼ *Staying in a caravan by the coast can provide an inexpensive seaside holiday. However, huge caravan parks can spoil the appearance of the coastline.*

SEA TRANSPORT

HUNDREDS OF INLETS AROUND THE COAST PROVIDE THE DEEP WATERS AND SHELTER NEEDED FOR SAFE HARBOURS AND PORTS. THE BIGGEST PORTS IN BRITAIN AND IRELAND DEVELOPED IN ESTUARIES.

SHIPS WERE ONCE the main method of long-distance transport for people, but nowadays aircraft have taken over. However, cruise-ship holidays are becoming increasingly popular. P&O has four cruise ships with another under construction. Ferries, hovercraft and high-speed catamarans are still used for carrying people and cargoes over shorter distances.

CARGOES

Millions of different products are transported around the world on cargo ships. But because of changes in the way cargo is transported, some ports have grown while others have declined.

Goods such as oil, corn, fertilisers and iron ore are now moved in huge bulk carriers or giant supertankers, which require deep water and special equipment for moving and handling their cargoes. A number of new specialist ports, such as Milford Haven or the Sullom Voe oil terminal, have been constructed to cope with the demand.

Instead of using thousands of boxes and sacks to package items, huge metal boxes, or containers, are now used. The containers are loaded with goods at the factory. Far fewer people are needed for this process, as it is largely mechanised.

ROLL-ON/ROLL-OFF SHIPS

The introduction of roll-on/roll-off ships has allowed lorries carrying cargo to drive directly on and off ships. To take one busy port as an example, roll-on/roll-off ferries, Hovercraft, bulk cargo and cruise ships operate from Dover, and all these methods of transport need their own facilities and equipment. Dover is a man-made harbour, with shelter provided by breakwaters. It is also the port nearest to France and the rest of Europe. However, even Dover is now suffering from competition from the Channel Tunnel. The Tunnel opened in 1994 but did not become fully operational until 1995. In 1994, Dover handled 19,123,743 passengers, 3,233,476 cars and 1,158,007 lorries. By 1999 these figures had

◄ *Giant cranes are used to load container ships at Tilbury Docks in the Thames estuary.*

◀ *A ferry prepares to leave the terminal in Dover for Calais in France.*

▶ *Customs officers use a specially trained dog to search cargo for smuggled drugs or other illegal substances.*

changed to 18,276,988 passengers, 3,003,364 cars and 1,667,942 lorries. The changes occurred despite the fact that a number of the long ferry crossings from the United Kingdom to mainland Europe had been discontinued.

PROTECTING THE PORTS

Around the coast, and particularly near ports, there are various methods of guiding ships safely into and out of harbours. Coastal waters can be extremely dangerous because of rocks and tides, and lighthouses and lightships send out a bright beam of light to warn ships of potential hazards. Navigation lights and buoys illuminate the correct channel for ships to

follow. Ports and the coastline are protected by people too. Coastguards – members of a government organisation – patrol the coast to prevent smuggling of goods and people, assist vessels in danger and watch out for oil pollution and other hazards.

PASSENGERS AND CARGO
- The most important cargo port in the British Isles is Felixstowe in Suffolk, which handles containers, lorries and bulk cargoes. Around 100 shipping lines use Felixstowe and visit 365 other ports. In 1999 it handled 31,465,860 tonnes of cargo.
- Dover is the busiest passenger port. In 1999, more than 18 million passengers passed through it.

POLLUTION

INCREASINGLY, PEOPLE ARE USING THE SEAS AROUND THE BRITISH ISLES AS A DUMPING GROUND FOR HUGE QUANTITIES OF RUBBISH, SEWAGE AND CHEMICALS, ENDANGERING PEOPLE AND WILDLIFE.

▲ *This sewage outfall pipe is on a salt marsh nature reserve in Hampshire.*

WHEN THE POPULATION of the British Isles was small and the waste people dumped into the sea was not usually poisonous, the sea could break down the waste materials and convert them to harmless substances. Today the population of the British Isles, at 62 million, is very high and we are producing huge amounts of waste, some of it very difficult, if not impossible, to decompose. Some of the waste is poisonous and a small amount is radioactive.

SEWAGE AND CHEMICAL POLLUTION

Human sewage from towns and cities is carried away through a drainage system to a sewage works, where it is usually treated. In many places on the coast, however, sewage is pumped straight into the sea. The action group Surfers Against Sewage claims that every day over 1300 million litres of sewage, much of it untreated, are discharged into the sea from sewage outfalls along our coastline. Some of the untreated sewage is later washed up on the shore. It spreads germs and also poisons shellfish, which are then eaten by people. Waste produced by farm animals contains more germs than the waste produced by people. The germs can easily be carried into rivers and streams, which eventually flow into the sea.

Many surfers and swimmers have been infected by germs in sea water, but no one knows how widespread the problem is. Many of the infections are minor and therefore not reported to doctors, and it isn't easy for the surfers and swimmers to prove exactly where they caught their infections.

Waste material from factories and power stations, including radioactive waste, is washed or drained into rivers. The rivers carry the waste to the sea, consequently poisoning birds, fish and other sea animals. Chemicals from rubbish dumps and farms can also seep into rivers and eventually the sea. It is estimated that two million tonnes of poisonous waste are discharged into the seas around the British Isles every year.

OIL POLLUTION

Half of the world's oil is transported at sea by supertankers and there have been a number of accidents. In 1993, 84,000 tonnes of oil spilled from the oil tanker *Braer* when it crashed in Shetland. Three years later, another tanker, *Sea Empress*, ran aground in Pembrokeshire and 72,000 tonnes of oil were spilled. Huge stretches of coastline were polluted and it is believed that 20,000 sea birds died.

▼ *Workmen clearing oil from a beach in Pembrokeshire after the* Sea Empress *ran aground in 1996.*

▲ *This herring gull has become trapped in a discarded nylon fishing line.*

▲ *Litter washed up on a beach at Gerrans Bay in Cornwall.*

Every year even larger quantities of oil are spilled from ships and rigs, or deliberately dumped. Sometimes detergents and other chemicals are used in an attempt to clean the oil from rocks, beaches and the sea. Many of these chemicals are poisonous and can be more harmful to sea animals and plants than the oil itself.

LITTER

Some people don't think about the consequences when they drop litter on beaches or over the side of a ship. Litter can be extremely dangerous. Broken glass and old medical syringes can cut people and spread infection. A discarded fishing net can trap and suffocate a seal or dolphin. A plastic canned-drink holder can strangle a bird. Surveys carried out show that more than half the litter on British beaches is made from plastic, which takes years to rot. Sometimes birds, fish and seals mistake pieces of plastic for food, swallow them and then either choke to death or die of starvation.

WILDLIFE HABITATS

ROCKY SHORES, SALT MARSHES, SAND DUNES, BEACHES AND
CLIFFS ARE ALL IMPORTANT HABITATS FOR WILDLIFE.

THE DEEPER, OPEN WATERS of the oceans and seas around the British Isles provide a comfortable environment for animals, as conditions do not change very much from day to day. However, the seashore changes dramatically every day as the tide rises and falls. The shore is sometimes wet and sometimes dry. It can be warmed by the sun or chilled by the wind and rain. The sea water itself varies; near estuaries it is diluted by river water. The salt content of the sea water also falls whenever it snows or rains. In hot, dry weather the water in rockpools becomes extremely salty. Every animal and plant along the coast is adapted to the conditions in which it lives; many are able to live partly in water and partly in air.

▼ *The wrasse is a common fish around the coasts of the British Isles, especially where there are cliffs and rocky shores. This wrasse has caught a lugworm in its powerful jaws.*

SAND AND SHINGLE

Only a few animals, such as razorfish, cockles, lugworms, fanworms and starfish are able to breathe whilst buried in the wet sand on a beach. When the tide comes in they become active and draw in water, sieving the food from it. A shingle beach, made up of constantly moving pebbles, is too dangerous for small animals, but some plants can live on this type of beach. Their long, deep roots hold them in place and absorb water from between the stones. They are able to withstand the strong, salty winds that blast around them throughout most of the year.

Many shore birds, including some gulls, terns, oystercatchers and ringed plovers, nest and breed on secluded shingle beaches. Dungeness in Kent and Orford Beach and Shingle Street in Suffolk are examples of shingle beaches that are home to a variety of

plant and animal life. Seaweeds cannot survive on sand and shingle because they are constantly shifting. But on rocky shores, they can stick to boulders and withstand being lashed about by the waves. Some types of seaweed can tolerate being exposed to the air at low tide for several hours each day. In some parts of Britain people eat seaweed, because it is rich in minerals. In western Ireland, people cook a common seaweed called carragheen or 'Irish moss', and in south-west Wales, people eat another common seaweed called laver.

LIFE IN ROCKPOOLS

A huge variety of animals and plants live in rockpools where they are sheltered from the waves. Barnacles, sea anemones, limpets and periwinkles cling to the rocks. They feed when the tide comes in. Fish such as blennies and pipefish live in the water amongst the seaweeds, whilst shrimps, starfish, crabs and hermit crabs shelter under the rocks.

SAND DUNES AND CLIFFS

In spite of their barren appearance, sand dunes, as soon as they have been colonised by plants, are rich in wildlife. Rabbits, field voles, wood mice, natterjack toads, lizards, banded snails and various butterflies live or feed on them. Gulls, terns, skylarks and shelduck often nest on them.

Very few cliffs are completely smooth. They usually have small ledges where plants can grow and on which birds can perch. Colonies of sea birds make their nests and raise their young on the cliffs, where their eggs are usually safe. Although birds nest and breed on cliffs, they obtain their food, like other sea birds, from the sea.

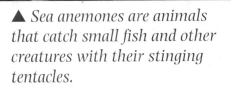

▲ *Sea anemones are animals that catch small fish and other creatures with their stinging tentacles.*

▶ *A colony of nesting gannets on Bass Rock, a rocky island in the Firth of Forth. They dive into the sea to catch fish.*

ESTUARIES

ESTUARIES ARE POPULAR SITES
FOR PORTS, POWER STATIONS
AND FACTORIES AND IMPORTANT
HABITATS FOR FISH, SHELLFISH
AND OTHER FORMS OF WILDLIFE.

AN ESTUARY IS THE PLACE where the valley of a river widens into a stretch of open water as it reaches the sea. As the river meets the tides and currents of the sea, it slows down and drops the mud and sand it has brought down from inland. The sea water carries away much of this sediment, but in sheltered estuaries some of the mud and sand builds up to form salt marshes. Plant seeds are carried to the salt marshes by the tides. As they grow, the plants trap mud and sand and, gradually, the level of the marsh rises. After hundreds of years, dry land forms.

ESTUARIES AND PORTS

There are more than 150 large estuaries around the British Isles, making up nearly half of the total coastline. Sheltered from the main force of the waves and tides, estuaries provide excellent sites for ports and marinas. The biggest ports of Britain and Ireland developed in the estuaries of rivers such as the Thames, Mersey, Clyde, Humber, Severn, Southampton Water, Lagan and Liffey.

As a port develops, so too do the industries and oil refineries that use the port. Because of the ready supply of cooling water, estuaries are popular sites for power stations. Barrages, such as the Thames Barrier and those on the Tees and across Cardiff Bay, are built on estuaries to prevent flooding further up the river.

▶ *Milford Haven in Pembrokeshire is the base for one of the largest oil ports in Europe and a site for marinas.*

▲ *The estuary of the River Alde in Suffolk has not been affected by development. The salt marshes are important feeding grounds for wildlife.*

NEW LAND

Because the water is shallow at the edge of an estuary, it is fairly easy to build walls or banks to keep out the sea, which creates valuable new land for farming or industry. Land has been 'reclaimed' around Wexford Harbour in Ireland and from estuaries in the Wash, Morecambe Bay, the Solway Firth and Romney Marsh in Kent.

▲ *The avocet, with its long legs and long curved beak, can easily search out small animals living in the mud and salt marshes.*

▶ *Many wading birds and wildfowl, like these greylag geese, feed and rest on estuaries during the winter months when food is scarce elsewhere.*

PLANNING PROBLEMS

An estuary may appear to be nothing more than a mass of mud with little or no wildlife. In fact, estuaries are the home for a wide variety of wildlife. Millions of worms, crabs and other small animals that can survive in both sea water and fresh water live in the thick layer of mud in an estuary. Fish feed on these creatures at high tide and ducks, geese and wading birds feed on them at low tide.

Some estuaries are internationally important – the Severn estuary, the Cheshire Dee, Morecambe Bay, the Solway, the Wash, North Bull near Dublin and Wexford Harbour – as places where thousands of wading birds and wildfowl rest and feed over the winter months. Estuaries are threatened by pollution and development. Some of the fish and shellfish we eat come from estuaries, yet pollution threatens that food supply. Many estuaries have been destroyed already; the remaining ones are crowded with birds and other animals struggling to find enough food to survive.

THE TEES ESTUARY

The story of the River Tees highlights the conflicting pressures on an estuary. The Tees rises in the Pennines and flows to the North Sea over a course of about 160 kilometres. Until fairly recently, the upper reaches of the river were polluted by farm chemicals and sewage from the towns along its banks. As the river approached its estuary, there was even more pollution from steel-making and chemical industries. The various ports along the estuary contributed to the pollution. Over the last 30 years, the older ports have closed down and a major new port, Teesport, has been constructed. New non-polluting industries have taken over some of the redundant ports and industrial buildings. A barrage has been built across the river to prevent flooding and to improve water quality. As a result of the changes, and because of the introduction of tougher new laws on pollution, the wildlife is again returning to the estuary. A survey by scientists from the Environment Agency in the year 2000 showed that thousands of sea trout and salmon were heading up river – a sure sign that the water quality is improving.

THE FUTURE OF OUR COASTS

As the population increases and as large numbers of tourists continue to flock to the sea, the pressures on our coasts will grow.

THE DEMAND FOR second homes, holiday camps, hotels, caravan sites, amusement parks, yacht marinas and dinghy parks is increasing. Many elderly people retire to coastal towns, which increases the demand for new houses. Industry near estuaries and ports continues to expand. About 31 per cent of the coastline of England and Wales is already occupied by buildings, roads, caravan parks, camping sites, car parks and golf courses. About 40 per cent of the United Kingdom's manufacturing industry is situated on or near the coast because of the easy access to ports.

CREATING ZONES

There is conflict between those who want to use the sea and beaches for quiet recreation and those people who want to take part in exciting, but noisy and disruptive activities such as water-skiing, jet-skiing, trail-bike riding and four-wheel drives on the beaches and dunes. One solution is to divide the coast into zones in which different activities are permitted. Some resorts are experimenting with this idea. Poole Harbour in Dorset is one of the world's largest natural harbours. It is a site of international importance for wildlife, but it is also used for watersports such as sailing, windsurfing, motor-boating and jet-skiing. Cross-channel ferries, cargo ships and fishing vessels also use the harbour, but around it are some popular holiday beaches. By dividing the harbour into zones for watersports and areas for quiet recreation, conflict between tourists has been reduced.

◀ *Watersports such as jet-skiing and surfing are popular pastimes in coastal waters.*

ORGANISATIONS

A number of organisations are working hard to protect the unspoiled parts of the coastline of the British Isles. The National Trust, the National Trust for Scotland and the National Trust for Ireland are funded by their members and through voluntary gifts. They have bought long stretches of attractive coastline and many historic sites with the proceeds. In addition, the government has made it more difficult for some parts of the coast to be developed by declaring them Areas of Outstanding Natural Beauty (AONB) or national parks. Many unspoiled areas of the coast are nature reserves and are owned or managed by organisations that will safeguard them. In a few places, parts of the coast below low water mark are protected as marine nature reserves. However, there are still many beautiful and interesting parts of our coasts that have no legal protection at all.

POLLUTION

There are already laws in place to prevent ships from deliberately dumping oil at sea, although it is not easy to catch the culprits who still do this. And, as we know, accidents can and do happen. There are also laws against dropping litter, but, again, they are not easy to enforce.

Several pressure groups, such as Greenpeace, the Marine Conservation Society and Surfers Against Sewage, are working hard to force the water companies to treat sewage before it is pumped into the sea and to ensure that factories and power stations do not pollute rivers and estuaries. Some urge their supporters to write to members of parliament and government ministers to encourage them to persuade the water companies to spend more of their profits on building efficient sewage treatment works.

Every year the European Union awards the cleanest beaches in Europe 'Blue Flags' in an attempt to persuade other resorts to clean up their coastline. There are no direct penalties for resorts that do not clean up their beaches. However, people are most likely to want to spend holidays at seaside resorts with clean, safe beaches and bathing waters. Resorts that don't tackle the problem will suffer financially.

◀ *In the year 2000, the UK was awarded 57 Blue Flag beaches. This showed a slight increase on the previous year.*

GLOSSARY

archipelago a group of islands formed when the sea level rises, leaving only the tops of mountains above the sea

backwash the movement of water in retreating waves

bar a ridge of sand or shingle across a bay or river mouth

barrage a barrier built across the mouth of a river to reduce the flow of water or to prevent flooding by the sea

bulk cargo one type of cargo carried in the hold of a ship

carboniferous the name given to a period in geological history about 345 million years ago when tropical conditions existed in Britain

cliff a steep rock face

container ship a ship that carries its cargo in large metal boxes, or containers

cultural tourism tourism based on the culture (i.e. theatre, art, etc.) of the place being visited or promoted

current the movement of sea water in a particular direction

erode to wear away the land by wind, moving water or ice

estuary the wide mouth of a river where fresh water meets sea water

fjord a Norwegian word meaning an inlet of the sea between high cliffs

global warming (or greenhouse effect) the warming of the Earth caused by gases from power stations, factories and motor vehicles

gneiss a coarse-grained rock

heritage tourism tourism based on places, objects or ideas from the past, eg. castles and museums

Ice Age a time when the land was covered in ice; it began about a million years ago and ended about 10,000 years ago

mainland the main part of a country, not the islands around it

pillbox a small, round fortification used for the positioning of weapons

pollution the harmful waste material from our homes, cars, factories, farms and power stations that dirties the air, soil, rivers and seas around us

port a place where ships stop to load and unload their cargo

salt marsh an area of wet land fed by salt water

sediment ground-down pieces of rock and other material carried along by a river

sewage the waste material and liquid from houses and factories, carried away by drains and sewers

silt sediment that has been ground down to form mud, clay or sand

spit a ridge of sand or shingle joined to the land at one end and extending into the sea at the other

sustainable capable of being continued indefinitely

tides the rise and fall of the oceans and seas twice each day

INDEX

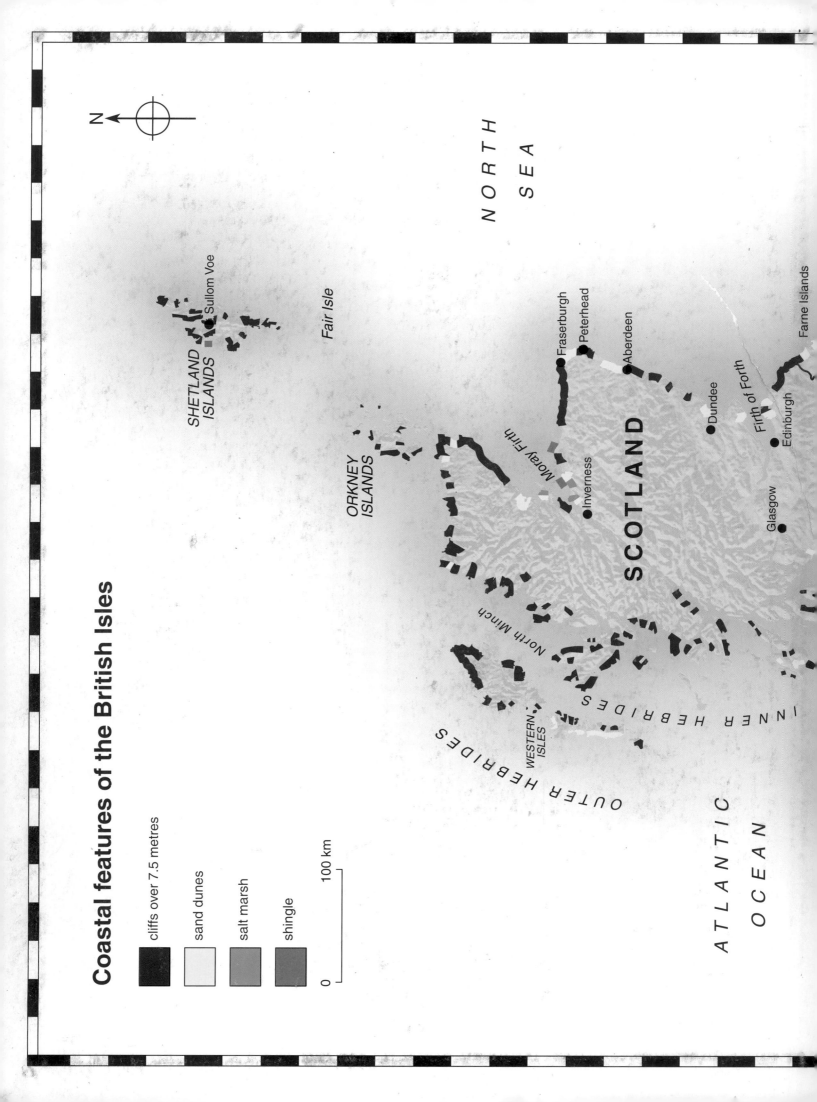

Coastal features of the British Isles

cliffs over 7.5 metres

sand dunes

salt marsh

shingle

0 ____ 100 km

N

NORTH SEA

ATLANTIC OCEAN

SHETLAND ISLANDS

Sullom Voe

Fair Isle

ORKNEY ISLANDS

SCOTLAND

Moray Firth

North Minch

WESTERN ISLES

OUTER HEBRIDES

INNER HEBRIDES

Fraserburgh

Peterhead

Aberdeen

Inverness

Dundee

Firth of Forth

Edinburgh

Glasgow

Farne Islands